50 Intermittent Fasting Recipes for Home

By: Kelly Johnson

Table of Contents

- Grilled Chicken Salad with Balsamic Vinaigrette
- Quinoa and Black Bean Stuffed Bell Peppers
- Mediterranean Tuna Salad
- Egg and Avocado Breakfast Wrap
- Cauliflower Rice Stir-Fry with Tofu
- Lemon Garlic Shrimp with Zucchini Noodles
- Greek Yogurt Parfait with Berries and Almonds
- Lentil Soup with Spinach and Tomatoes
- Turkey and Veggie Lettuce Wraps
- Sweet Potato and Black Bean Chili
- Salmon with Roasted Asparagus
- Vegan Buddha Bowl with Roasted Veggies and Quinoa
- Chicken and Vegetable Skewers with Peanut Sauce
- Spinach and Feta Omelette
- Cauliflower Crust Pizza with Chicken and Pesto
- Greek Chicken Souvlaki with Tzatziki Sauce
- Turkey Meatballs with Marinara Sauce
- Coconut Chia Seed Pudding with Mango
- Avocado and Tomato Salad with Lime Dressing
- Sautéed Shrimp with Garlic and Broccoli
- Quinoa Salad with Cucumber and Mint
- Eggplant Parmesan with Marinara Sauce
- Mexican Cauliflower Rice Bowl
- Baked Cod with Lemon and Herbs
- Chickpea Salad with Cucumber and Red Onion
- Turkey and Vegetable Stir-Fry
- Caprese Salad with Balsamic Glaze
- Stuffed Portobello Mushrooms with Spinach and Goat Cheese
- Chicken Lettuce Cups with Asian Sauce
- Ratatouille with Quinoa
- Greek Yogurt Chicken Salad with Grapes and Walnuts
- Veggie Frittata with Sweet Potato Crust
- Shrimp and Avocado Salad with Lime Dressing
- Lentil and Vegetable Curry
- Turkey and Quinoa Stuffed Bell Peppers

- Spaghetti Squash with Turkey Meatballs
- Greek Lemon Chicken Soup
- Cauliflower Fried Rice with Chicken and Vegetables
- Black Bean and Corn Salad with Cilantro Lime Dressing
- Grilled Salmon with Asparagus and Lemon Dill Sauce
- Mediterranean Chickpea Salad with Feta
- Tofu and Veggie Stir-Fry with Ginger Sauce
- Egg Salad Lettuce Wraps
- Roasted Vegetable Quinoa Bowl
- Turkey Chili with Butternut Squash
- Baked Chicken with Brussels Sprouts and Bacon
- Greek Quinoa Stuffed Peppers
- Spinach and Mushroom Omelette
- Vegan Coconut Curry with Tofu
- Grilled Vegetable Skewers with Pesto Dipping Sauce

Grilled Chicken Salad with Balsamic Vinaigrette

Ingredients:

- 2 boneless, skinless chicken breasts
- Salt and pepper to taste
- 6 cups mixed salad greens (such as lettuce, spinach, arugula)
- 1 cup cherry tomatoes, halved
- 1 cucumber, sliced
- 1/4 red onion, thinly sliced
- 1/4 cup crumbled feta cheese
- 1/4 cup chopped walnuts (optional)

For the Balsamic Vinaigrette:

- 1/4 cup balsamic vinegar
- 1/2 cup extra virgin olive oil
- 1 tablespoon Dijon mustard
- 1 clove garlic, minced
- Salt and pepper to taste

Instructions:

1. Preheat grill to medium-high heat.
2. Season chicken breasts with salt and pepper on both sides.
3. Grill chicken for 6-7 minutes per side, or until cooked through and no longer pink in the center. Remove from grill and let rest for 5 minutes before slicing.
4. In a small bowl, whisk together balsamic vinegar, olive oil, Dijon mustard, minced garlic, salt, and pepper to make the vinaigrette.
5. In a large salad bowl, combine mixed greens, cherry tomatoes, cucumber slices, and red onion slices.
6. Add sliced grilled chicken on top of the salad.
7. Drizzle balsamic vinaigrette over the salad and toss gently to coat.
8. Sprinkle crumbled feta cheese and chopped walnuts (if using) over the salad.
9. Serve immediately and enjoy!

Quinoa and Black Bean Stuffed Bell Peppers

Ingredients:

- 4 large bell peppers, any color
- 1 cup quinoa, rinsed
- 2 cups vegetable broth or water
- 1 tablespoon olive oil
- 1 small onion, diced
- 2 cloves garlic, minced
- 1 can (15 ounces) black beans, drained and rinsed
- 1 can (14.5 ounces) diced tomatoes, drained
- 1 cup corn kernels (fresh, frozen, or canned)
- 1 teaspoon ground cumin
- 1 teaspoon chili powder
- Salt and pepper to taste
- 1 cup shredded cheese (cheddar, Monterey Jack, or a blend), optional
- Fresh cilantro, chopped, for garnish

Instructions:

1. Preheat your oven to 375°F (190°C).
2. Cut the tops off the bell peppers and remove the seeds and membranes. Place the peppers cut side up in a baking dish and set aside.
3. In a medium saucepan, combine quinoa and vegetable broth (or water). Bring to a boil, then reduce heat to low, cover, and simmer for about 15 minutes, or until quinoa is cooked and liquid is absorbed. Remove from heat and fluff with a fork.
4. In a large skillet, heat olive oil over medium heat. Add diced onion and cook until softened, about 5 minutes. Add minced garlic and cook for another minute until fragrant.
5. Stir in black beans, diced tomatoes, corn kernels, cooked quinoa, ground cumin, chili powder, salt, and pepper. Cook for 5-7 minutes, stirring occasionally, until heated through and flavors are combined.
6. Spoon the quinoa and black bean mixture into the hollowed-out bell peppers until they are filled to the top.
7. If using cheese, sprinkle shredded cheese over the top of each stuffed bell pepper.

8. Cover the baking dish with aluminum foil and bake in the preheated oven for 25-30 minutes, or until the peppers are tender.
9. Remove the foil and bake for an additional 5 minutes, or until cheese is melted and bubbly (if using).
10. Remove from the oven and let cool for a few minutes before serving.
11. Garnish with fresh chopped cilantro before serving, if desired.
12. Enjoy your delicious quinoa and black bean stuffed bell peppers!

Mediterranean Tuna Salad

Ingredients:

- 2 cans (5 ounces each) tuna, drained
- 1/2 cup cherry tomatoes, halved
- 1/4 cup Kalamata olives, pitted and sliced
- 1/4 cup diced red onion
- 1/4 cup diced cucumber
- 1/4 cup diced red bell pepper
- 2 tablespoons chopped fresh parsley
- 2 tablespoons chopped fresh basil
- 2 tablespoons extra virgin olive oil
- 1 tablespoon lemon juice
- 1 clove garlic, minced
- Salt and pepper to taste
- Optional: crumbled feta cheese, for garnish

Instructions:

1. In a large mixing bowl, combine the drained tuna, cherry tomatoes, Kalamata olives, diced red onion, diced cucumber, diced red bell pepper, chopped fresh parsley, and chopped fresh basil.
2. In a small bowl, whisk together the extra virgin olive oil, lemon juice, minced garlic, salt, and pepper to make the dressing.
3. Pour the dressing over the tuna mixture in the large bowl and toss gently to coat all ingredients evenly.
4. Taste and adjust seasoning with more salt and pepper if needed.
5. If desired, sprinkle crumbled feta cheese over the top of the salad before serving.
6. Serve the Mediterranean tuna salad immediately, or chill it in the refrigerator for about 30 minutes to let the flavors meld together.
7. Enjoy your refreshing and flavorful Mediterranean tuna salad as a light meal or as a filling for sandwiches or wraps!

Egg and Avocado Breakfast Wrap

Ingredients:

- 2 large eggs
- 1 large whole wheat or spinach tortilla
- 1/2 avocado, sliced
- 1/4 cup diced tomatoes
- 2 tablespoons diced red onion
- 1/4 cup shredded cheese (such as cheddar or Monterey Jack)
- Salt and pepper to taste
- Optional: hot sauce or salsa for serving

Instructions:

1. In a small bowl, beat the eggs with a pinch of salt and pepper until well mixed.
2. Heat a non-stick skillet over medium heat. Pour the beaten eggs into the skillet and cook, stirring occasionally, until scrambled and cooked through.
3. Place the tortilla on a flat surface. Arrange the sliced avocado in the center of the tortilla, leaving some space around the edges.
4. Spoon the scrambled eggs on top of the avocado slices.
5. Sprinkle diced tomatoes and diced red onion over the scrambled eggs.
6. Sprinkle shredded cheese evenly over the filling.
7. Optional: Drizzle hot sauce or salsa over the filling for extra flavor.
8. Fold the sides of the tortilla over the filling, then roll it up tightly to form a wrap.
9. Serve the egg and avocado breakfast wrap immediately, or wrap it in foil for an on-the-go meal.
10. Enjoy your delicious and satisfying breakfast wrap!

Cauliflower Rice Stir-Fry with Tofu

Ingredients:

- 1 medium head of cauliflower, riced (or approximately 4 cups pre-riced cauliflower)
- 1 block (14-ounce) firm tofu, drained and cubed
- 2 tablespoons soy sauce (or tamari for gluten-free option)
- 1 tablespoon sesame oil
- 2 tablespoons vegetable oil
- 2 cloves garlic, minced
- 1 tablespoon minced ginger
- 1 cup mixed vegetables (such as bell peppers, carrots, snap peas, broccoli)
- Salt and pepper to taste
- Optional toppings: sliced green onions, sesame seeds

Instructions:

1. If you haven't already, rice the cauliflower by cutting it into florets and pulsing in a food processor until it resembles rice. Alternatively, you can use pre-riced cauliflower from the store.
2. In a small bowl, mix together the soy sauce and sesame oil. Set aside.
3. Heat 1 tablespoon of vegetable oil in a large skillet or wok over medium-high heat. Add the cubed tofu and cook until golden brown on all sides, about 5-7 minutes. Remove tofu from the skillet and set aside.
4. In the same skillet, add the remaining tablespoon of vegetable oil. Add minced garlic and minced ginger, and cook for about 1 minute until fragrant.
5. Add the mixed vegetables to the skillet and stir-fry for 3-4 minutes until they are tender-crisp.
6. Push the vegetables to one side of the skillet and add the riced cauliflower to the empty space. Cook for 3-4 minutes, stirring occasionally, until the cauliflower is tender.
7. Return the cooked tofu to the skillet and pour the soy sauce mixture over the tofu and cauliflower. Stir everything together until well combined and heated through.
8. Season with salt and pepper to taste.
9. Remove from heat and transfer the cauliflower rice stir-fry with tofu to serving plates.

10. Garnish with sliced green onions and sesame seeds, if desired.
11. Serve hot and enjoy your flavorful and nutritious cauliflower rice stir-fry with tofu!

Greek Yogurt Parfait with Berries and Almonds

Ingredients:

- 1 cup Greek yogurt (plain or flavored, such as vanilla)
- 1/2 cup mixed berries (such as strawberries, blueberries, raspberries)
- 2 tablespoons sliced almonds
- 1 tablespoon honey or maple syrup (optional)
- Granola (optional, for added crunch)

Instructions:

1. In a serving glass or bowl, start by layering about 1/4 cup of Greek yogurt at the bottom.
2. Add a layer of mixed berries on top of the yogurt.
3. Sprinkle a tablespoon of sliced almonds over the berries.
4. Repeat the layers with another 1/4 cup of Greek yogurt, more mixed berries, and sliced almonds until the glass or bowl is filled.
5. If desired, drizzle a tablespoon of honey or maple syrup over the top layer for added sweetness.
6. Optional: Add a layer of granola between the yogurt and berries for extra crunch and texture.
7. Serve the Greek yogurt parfait immediately, or cover and refrigerate until ready to eat.
8. Enjoy your delicious and nutritious Greek yogurt parfait with berries and almonds as a breakfast, snack, or dessert!

Lentil Soup with Spinach and Tomatoes

Ingredients:

- 1 cup dried lentils (any variety), rinsed and drained
- 1 tablespoon olive oil
- 1 onion, diced
- 2 cloves garlic, minced
- 2 carrots, diced
- 2 stalks celery, diced
- 1 can (14.5 ounces) diced tomatoes
- 4 cups vegetable broth
- 2 cups fresh spinach leaves, chopped
- 1 teaspoon dried thyme
- 1 teaspoon dried oregano
- Salt and pepper to taste
- Fresh lemon juice (optional, for serving)
- Fresh parsley, chopped (optional, for garnish)

Instructions:

1. In a large pot or Dutch oven, heat the olive oil over medium heat. Add the diced onion and cook until softened, about 5 minutes.
2. Add the minced garlic and cook for an additional minute until fragrant.
3. Stir in the diced carrots and celery, and cook for another 5 minutes until slightly softened.
4. Add the rinsed lentils, diced tomatoes (with their juices), vegetable broth, dried thyme, and dried oregano to the pot. Stir to combine.
5. Bring the soup to a boil, then reduce the heat to low and simmer, covered, for about 20-25 minutes, or until the lentils are tender.
6. Once the lentils are cooked, stir in the chopped spinach leaves and cook for another 2-3 minutes until wilted.
7. Season the lentil soup with salt and pepper to taste.
8. If desired, add a squeeze of fresh lemon juice to brighten the flavors.
9. Ladle the lentil soup into bowls and garnish with chopped fresh parsley, if desired.

10. Serve hot and enjoy your comforting and nutritious lentil soup with spinach and tomatoes!

Turkey and Veggie Lettuce Wraps

Ingredients:

- 1 lb ground turkey
- 1 tablespoon olive oil
- 1 onion, finely diced
- 2 cloves garlic, minced
- 1 red bell pepper, finely diced
- 1 carrot, grated
- 1 zucchini, grated
- 1 teaspoon ground cumin
- 1 teaspoon chili powder
- Salt and pepper to taste
- 1/4 cup hoisin sauce
- 2 tablespoons soy sauce
- 2 tablespoons chopped fresh cilantro
- 1 head iceberg or butter lettuce, leaves separated

Instructions:

1. Heat olive oil in a large skillet over medium heat. Add the diced onion and cook until softened, about 3-4 minutes.
2. Add minced garlic and cook for an additional minute until fragrant.
3. Add the ground turkey to the skillet, breaking it apart with a spatula. Cook until browned and cooked through, about 5-7 minutes.
4. Stir in the diced red bell pepper, grated carrot, and grated zucchini. Cook for 3-4 minutes until vegetables are softened.
5. Add the ground cumin, chili powder, salt, and pepper to the skillet. Stir to combine.
6. Pour in the hoisin sauce and soy sauce, stirring well to coat the turkey and vegetables. Cook for another 2-3 minutes until heated through.
7. Remove the skillet from heat and stir in the chopped fresh cilantro.
8. To serve, spoon the turkey and vegetable mixture onto individual lettuce leaves, using them as wraps.
9. Optional: Serve with additional hoisin sauce or sriracha on the side for dipping.
10. Enjoy your flavorful and healthy turkey and veggie lettuce wraps as a light and satisfying meal!

Sweet Potato and Black Bean Chili

Ingredients:

- 2 tablespoons olive oil
- 1 onion, diced
- 2 cloves garlic, minced
- 1 large sweet potato, peeled and diced
- 1 red bell pepper, diced
- 1 can (15 ounces) black beans, drained and rinsed
- 1 can (14.5 ounces) diced tomatoes
- 2 cups vegetable broth
- 1 tablespoon chili powder
- 1 teaspoon ground cumin
- 1/2 teaspoon paprika
- Salt and pepper to taste
- Optional toppings: chopped fresh cilantro, sliced green onions, shredded cheese, avocado slices, sour cream

Instructions:

1. Heat olive oil in a large pot over medium heat. Add the diced onion and cook until softened, about 5 minutes.
2. Add minced garlic and cook for an additional minute until fragrant.
3. Add diced sweet potato and diced red bell pepper to the pot. Cook for 5-7 minutes, stirring occasionally, until vegetables start to soften.
4. Stir in the drained and rinsed black beans, diced tomatoes (with their juices), vegetable broth, chili powder, ground cumin, paprika, salt, and pepper.
5. Bring the chili to a boil, then reduce the heat to low and simmer, covered, for about 20-25 minutes, or until the sweet potatoes are tender.
6. Taste and adjust seasoning with more salt and pepper if needed.
7. If desired, mash some of the sweet potatoes and black beans with the back of a spoon to thicken the chili.
8. Ladle the sweet potato and black bean chili into bowls and serve hot.
9. Garnish with chopped fresh cilantro, sliced green onions, shredded cheese, avocado slices, and/or sour cream, if desired.

10. Enjoy your hearty and flavorful sweet potato and black bean chili on a cold day or any time you're craving a comforting meal!

Salmon with Roasted Asparagus

Ingredients:

- 4 salmon fillets
- 1 bunch asparagus, trimmed
- 2 tablespoons olive oil
- 2 cloves garlic, minced
- 1 lemon, sliced
- Salt and pepper to taste
- Optional garnish: chopped fresh parsley, grated Parmesan cheese

Instructions:

1. Preheat your oven to 400°F (200°C).
2. Place the trimmed asparagus spears on a baking sheet. Drizzle with olive oil and minced garlic, then toss to coat the asparagus evenly. Season with salt and pepper to taste.
3. Arrange the lemon slices on top of the asparagus.
4. Place the salmon fillets on the same baking sheet, next to the asparagus. Drizzle the salmon with a little olive oil and season with salt and pepper.
5. Place the baking sheet in the preheated oven and roast for about 12-15 minutes, or until the salmon is cooked through and flakes easily with a fork, and the asparagus is tender but still slightly crisp.
6. Once cooked, remove the baking sheet from the oven.
7. Transfer the salmon fillets and roasted asparagus to serving plates.
8. Optional: Garnish the salmon with chopped fresh parsley and grated Parmesan cheese for extra flavor.
9. Serve hot, with additional lemon slices on the side if desired.
10. Enjoy your delicious and nutritious salmon with roasted asparagus for a satisfying and healthy meal!

Vegan Buddha Bowl with Roasted Veggies and Quinoa

Ingredients:

For the Roasted Veggies:

- 2 cups mixed vegetables (such as broccoli florets, cauliflower florets, bell peppers, carrots, zucchini), chopped into bite-sized pieces
- 2 tablespoons olive oil
- 1 teaspoon garlic powder
- 1 teaspoon paprika
- Salt and pepper to taste

For the Quinoa:

- 1 cup quinoa, rinsed
- 2 cups vegetable broth or water

For the Lemon-Tahini Dressing:

- 1/4 cup tahini
- 2 tablespoons lemon juice
- 2 tablespoons water
- 1 clove garlic, minced
- Salt and pepper to taste

For Assembly:

- 2 cups cooked chickpeas (canned or cooked from dried)
- 2 cups baby spinach or mixed greens
- 1 avocado, sliced
- Optional garnish: sesame seeds, chopped fresh herbs (such as parsley or cilantro)

Instructions:

1. Preheat your oven to 400°F (200°C).
2. In a large bowl, toss the mixed vegetables with olive oil, garlic powder, paprika, salt, and pepper until evenly coated.
3. Spread the seasoned vegetables in a single layer on a baking sheet lined with parchment paper.
4. Roast the vegetables in the preheated oven for 20-25 minutes, or until tender and lightly browned, stirring halfway through cooking.
5. While the vegetables are roasting, prepare the quinoa. In a saucepan, combine the rinsed quinoa and vegetable broth (or water). Bring to a boil, then reduce heat to low, cover, and simmer for about 15 minutes, or until the quinoa is cooked and liquid is absorbed. Remove from heat and let it sit covered for 5 minutes, then fluff with a fork.
6. In a small bowl, whisk together the tahini, lemon juice, water, minced garlic, salt, and pepper until smooth and creamy. Adjust consistency by adding more water if needed.
7. To assemble the Buddha bowls, divide the cooked quinoa among serving bowls. Arrange the roasted veggies, cooked chickpeas, baby spinach or mixed greens, and avocado slices on top of the quinoa.
8. Drizzle each bowl with the lemon-tahini dressing.
9. Optional: Garnish with sesame seeds and chopped fresh herbs.
10. Serve immediately and enjoy your nourishing and flavorful vegan Buddha bowls with roasted veggies and quinoa!

Chicken and Vegetable Skewers with Peanut Sauce

Ingredients:

For the Chicken and Vegetable Skewers:

- 1 lb boneless, skinless chicken breasts, cut into cubes
- 2 bell peppers, cut into chunks
- 1 zucchini, sliced into rounds
- 1 red onion, cut into chunks
- Wooden or metal skewers (if using wooden skewers, soak them in water for 30 minutes before using)

For the Marinade:

- 1/4 cup soy sauce
- 2 tablespoons olive oil
- 2 cloves garlic, minced
- 1 teaspoon ground ginger
- 1 tablespoon honey or maple syrup (optional)
- Salt and pepper to taste

For the Peanut Sauce:

- 1/4 cup creamy peanut butter
- 2 tablespoons soy sauce
- 1 tablespoon rice vinegar
- 1 tablespoon maple syrup or honey
- 1 clove garlic, minced
- 1 teaspoon grated ginger
- 1-2 tablespoons water (adjust for desired consistency)
- Optional garnish: chopped peanuts, chopped cilantro, lime wedges

Instructions:

1. In a bowl, whisk together the ingredients for the marinade: soy sauce, olive oil, minced garlic, ground ginger, honey or maple syrup (if using), salt, and pepper.

2. Place the cubed chicken in a shallow dish or resealable plastic bag. Pour the marinade over the chicken, making sure it's evenly coated. Cover or seal and refrigerate for at least 30 minutes, or up to 4 hours.
3. While the chicken is marinating, prepare the peanut sauce. In a small bowl, whisk together the peanut butter, soy sauce, rice vinegar, maple syrup or honey, minced garlic, grated ginger, and water until smooth. Set aside.
4. Preheat your grill or grill pan to medium-high heat.
5. Thread the marinated chicken cubes, bell peppers, zucchini slices, and red onion chunks onto the skewers, alternating between the chicken and vegetables.
6. Grill the skewers for 8-10 minutes, turning occasionally, until the chicken is cooked through and the vegetables are tender and lightly charred.
7. Remove the skewers from the grill and transfer them to a serving platter.
8. Drizzle the chicken and vegetable skewers with the prepared peanut sauce.
9. Optional: Garnish with chopped peanuts, chopped cilantro, and lime wedges.
10. Serve immediately and enjoy your delicious chicken and vegetable skewers with peanut sauce!

Spinach and Feta Omelette

Ingredients:

- 2 large eggs
- 1 tablespoon milk or water
- Salt and pepper to taste
- 1 teaspoon olive oil or butter
- 1 cup fresh spinach leaves, roughly chopped
- 2 tablespoons crumbled feta cheese

Instructions:

1. In a small bowl, whisk together the eggs, milk or water, salt, and pepper until well combined.
2. Heat the olive oil or butter in a non-stick skillet over medium heat.
3. Add the chopped spinach to the skillet and sauté for 1-2 minutes until wilted.
4. Pour the beaten egg mixture into the skillet, swirling to evenly distribute the eggs.
5. Cook the omelette for 2-3 minutes, lifting the edges with a spatula and tilting the skillet to allow the uncooked egg to flow underneath.
6. Once the bottom is set and the top is still slightly runny, sprinkle crumbled feta cheese evenly over one half of the omelette.
7. Using a spatula, fold the other half of the omelette over the side with the cheese, forming a half-moon shape.
8. Cook for another 1-2 minutes until the cheese is melted and the omelette is cooked through.
9. Slide the omelette onto a plate and serve hot.
10. Optionally, garnish with additional feta cheese or fresh herbs like parsley or dill.
11. Enjoy your delicious spinach and feta omelette for breakfast or brunch!

Cauliflower Crust Pizza with Chicken and Pesto

Ingredients:

For the Cauliflower Crust:

- 1 medium head cauliflower, riced (about 4 cups)
- 1/2 cup shredded mozzarella cheese
- 1/4 cup grated Parmesan cheese
- 1 teaspoon Italian seasoning
- 1/2 teaspoon garlic powder
- 1/4 teaspoon salt
- 1 large egg, beaten

For the Toppings:

- 1/2 cup pesto sauce (store-bought or homemade)
- 1 cup cooked chicken breast, diced or shredded
- 1/2 cup cherry tomatoes, halved
- 1/4 cup sliced black olives
- 1/4 cup crumbled feta cheese (optional)
- Fresh basil leaves, for garnish (optional)

Instructions:

1. Preheat your oven to 425°F (220°C). Line a baking sheet with parchment paper or lightly grease it with olive oil.
2. Prepare the cauliflower crust by first ricing the cauliflower. You can do this by grating the cauliflower florets using a box grater or by pulsing them in a food processor until they resemble rice.
3. Place the riced cauliflower in a microwave-safe bowl and microwave on high for 5-6 minutes, until softened.
4. Once the cauliflower is cooked, allow it to cool for a few minutes, then transfer it to a clean kitchen towel or cheesecloth. Squeeze out as much excess moisture as possible.

5. In a large mixing bowl, combine the squeezed cauliflower, shredded mozzarella cheese, grated Parmesan cheese, Italian seasoning, garlic powder, salt, and beaten egg. Mix until well combined.
6. Transfer the cauliflower mixture to the prepared baking sheet. Using your hands, press the mixture into a thin, even layer, forming a circle or rectangle shape for the pizza crust.
7. Bake the cauliflower crust in the preheated oven for 15-20 minutes, or until golden brown and firm to the touch.
8. Remove the crust from the oven and let it cool slightly. Leave the oven on.
9. Once cooled, spread the pesto sauce evenly over the cauliflower crust, leaving a small border around the edges.
10. Arrange the cooked chicken breast, halved cherry tomatoes, and sliced black olives over the pesto sauce.
11. If using, sprinkle crumbled feta cheese over the top of the pizza.
12. Return the pizza to the oven and bake for an additional 8-10 minutes, or until the toppings are heated through and the cheese is melted and bubbly.
13. Remove the pizza from the oven and let it cool for a few minutes before slicing.
14. Garnish with fresh basil leaves, if desired, before serving.
15. Slice the cauliflower crust pizza into wedges or squares and enjoy your delicious and nutritious meal!

Greek Chicken Souvlaki with Tzatziki Sauce

Ingredients:

For the Chicken Souvlaki:

- 1 lb boneless, skinless chicken breasts, cut into cubes
- 2 tablespoons olive oil
- 2 tablespoons lemon juice
- 2 cloves garlic, minced
- 1 teaspoon dried oregano
- 1/2 teaspoon dried thyme
- Salt and pepper to taste
- Wooden or metal skewers

For the Tzatziki Sauce:

- 1 cup Greek yogurt
- 1/2 cucumber, grated and squeezed to remove excess moisture
- 1 clove garlic, minced
- 1 tablespoon lemon juice
- 1 tablespoon chopped fresh dill (or 1 teaspoon dried dill)
- Salt and pepper to taste

For Serving:

- Pita bread or flatbread
- Sliced tomatoes
- Sliced red onion
- Chopped fresh parsley or cilantro (optional)
- Lemon wedges

Instructions:

1. In a bowl, whisk together the olive oil, lemon juice, minced garlic, dried oregano, dried thyme, salt, and pepper to make the marinade.

2. Place the chicken cubes in a shallow dish or resealable plastic bag. Pour the marinade over the chicken, making sure it's evenly coated. Cover or seal and refrigerate for at least 30 minutes, or up to 4 hours.
3. While the chicken is marinating, prepare the tzatziki sauce. In a bowl, combine the Greek yogurt, grated cucumber, minced garlic, lemon juice, chopped fresh dill, salt, and pepper. Mix well, then cover and refrigerate until ready to serve.
4. If using wooden skewers, soak them in water for 30 minutes to prevent burning.
5. Preheat your grill or grill pan to medium-high heat.
6. Thread the marinated chicken cubes onto the skewers.
7. Grill the chicken skewers for 5-7 minutes per side, or until cooked through and lightly charred on the outside.
8. While the chicken is cooking, warm the pita bread or flatbread on the grill for a few minutes on each side.
9. Once the chicken is cooked, remove the skewers from the grill and let them rest for a few minutes.
10. To assemble, place a warm pita bread or flatbread on a plate. Top with sliced tomatoes and red onion.
11. Slide the grilled chicken off the skewers and onto the pita bread.
12. Drizzle with tzatziki sauce and sprinkle with chopped fresh parsley or cilantro, if desired.
13. Serve immediately with lemon wedges on the side.
14. Enjoy your delicious Greek chicken souvlaki with tzatziki sauce!

Turkey Meatballs with Marinara Sauce

Ingredients:

For the Turkey Meatballs:

- 1 lb ground turkey
- 1/2 cup breadcrumbs
- 1/4 cup grated Parmesan cheese
- 1 large egg
- 2 cloves garlic, minced
- 2 tablespoons chopped fresh parsley
- 1 teaspoon dried oregano
- 1/2 teaspoon salt
- 1/4 teaspoon black pepper
- 2 tablespoons olive oil, for cooking

For the Marinara Sauce:

- 1 tablespoon olive oil
- 1 onion, finely diced
- 2 cloves garlic, minced
- 1 can (14.5 ounces) crushed tomatoes
- 1 can (8 ounces) tomato sauce
- 1 teaspoon dried basil
- 1 teaspoon dried oregano
- 1/2 teaspoon dried thyme
- Salt and pepper to taste

Instructions:

1. Preheat your oven to 400°F (200°C).
2. In a large mixing bowl, combine the ground turkey, breadcrumbs, grated Parmesan cheese, egg, minced garlic, chopped fresh parsley, dried oregano, salt, and black pepper. Mix until well combined.
3. Shape the turkey mixture into meatballs, about 1 to 1.5 inches in diameter.

4. Heat 2 tablespoons of olive oil in a large skillet over medium heat. Add the meatballs in batches, making sure not to overcrowd the skillet. Cook for 2-3 minutes on each side, or until browned. Transfer the browned meatballs to a baking sheet lined with parchment paper.
5. Once all the meatballs are browned, transfer the baking sheet to the preheated oven. Bake for 10-12 minutes, or until the meatballs are cooked through.
6. While the meatballs are baking, prepare the marinara sauce. In the same skillet used for browning the meatballs, heat 1 tablespoon of olive oil over medium heat.
7. Add the finely diced onion to the skillet and cook until softened, about 5 minutes. Add the minced garlic and cook for an additional minute until fragrant.
8. Stir in the crushed tomatoes, tomato sauce, dried basil, dried oregano, dried thyme, salt, and pepper. Bring the sauce to a simmer and let it cook for 10-15 minutes, stirring occasionally, to allow the flavors to meld together.
9. Once the meatballs are cooked through, remove them from the oven and add them to the marinara sauce. Stir gently to coat the meatballs in the sauce.
10. Serve the turkey meatballs with marinara sauce hot, garnished with additional chopped parsley or grated Parmesan cheese if desired.
11. Enjoy your delicious and hearty turkey meatballs with marinara sauce!

Coconut Chia Seed Pudding with Mango

Ingredients:

- 1/4 cup chia seeds
- 1 cup coconut milk (canned or homemade)
- 1 tablespoon maple syrup or honey (optional, adjust to taste)
- 1/2 teaspoon vanilla extract
- 1 ripe mango, diced
- Shredded coconut, for garnish (optional)

Instructions:

1. In a bowl or jar, combine the chia seeds, coconut milk, maple syrup or honey (if using), and vanilla extract. Stir well to combine.
2. Cover the bowl or jar and refrigerate for at least 4 hours, or preferably overnight, to allow the chia seeds to absorb the liquid and thicken.
3. After the chia pudding has thickened to your desired consistency, give it a good stir to break up any clumps.
4. To serve, spoon the chia seed pudding into serving bowls or glasses.
5. Top the pudding with diced mango pieces.
6. If desired, sprinkle shredded coconut over the top for extra flavor and texture.
7. Serve immediately and enjoy your refreshing coconut chia seed pudding with mango!
8. Optionally, you can store any leftover pudding in an airtight container in the refrigerator for up to 3-4 days.

Avocado and Tomato Salad with Lime Dressing

Ingredients:

For the Salad:

- 2 ripe avocados, diced
- 2 large tomatoes, diced
- 1/4 cup red onion, finely chopped
- 2 tablespoons fresh cilantro or parsley, chopped
- Salt and pepper to taste
- Optional: crumbled feta cheese, sliced jalapeños, black beans, corn kernels

For the Lime Dressing:

- 3 tablespoons olive oil
- 2 tablespoons fresh lime juice
- 1 clove garlic, minced
- 1 teaspoon honey or maple syrup (optional)
- 1/2 teaspoon ground cumin
- Salt and pepper to taste

Instructions:

1. In a large bowl, combine the diced avocados, diced tomatoes, chopped red onion, and chopped cilantro or parsley.
2. If using any optional ingredients like crumbled feta cheese, sliced jalapeños, black beans, or corn kernels, add them to the salad as well.
3. In a small bowl, whisk together the olive oil, fresh lime juice, minced garlic, honey or maple syrup (if using), ground cumin, salt, and pepper to make the lime dressing.
4. Pour the lime dressing over the avocado and tomato salad.
5. Gently toss the salad until all ingredients are evenly coated with the dressing.
6. Taste and adjust seasoning with more salt, pepper, or lime juice if needed.
7. Serve the avocado and tomato salad immediately, or refrigerate for 15-30 minutes to let the flavors meld together before serving.

8. Enjoy your refreshing and flavorful avocado and tomato salad with lime dressing as a side dish or light meal!

Sautéed Shrimp with Garlic and Broccoli

Ingredients:

- 1 lb large shrimp, peeled and deveined
- 2 cups broccoli florets
- 4 cloves garlic, minced
- 2 tablespoons olive oil
- 2 tablespoons butter
- Salt and pepper to taste
- Red pepper flakes (optional, for heat)
- Lemon wedges for serving

Instructions:

1. Pat the shrimp dry with paper towels and season with salt and pepper.
2. Heat 1 tablespoon of olive oil in a large skillet over medium-high heat.
3. Add the broccoli florets to the skillet and sauté for 3-4 minutes, or until they start to soften. Remove the broccoli from the skillet and set aside.
4. In the same skillet, add the remaining tablespoon of olive oil and the butter. Once the butter has melted, add the minced garlic and red pepper flakes (if using). Sauté for about 1 minute until fragrant.
5. Add the seasoned shrimp to the skillet in a single layer. Cook for 2-3 minutes on each side, or until the shrimp are pink and opaque.
6. Return the sautéed broccoli to the skillet with the cooked shrimp. Toss everything together until the shrimp and broccoli are evenly coated with the garlic butter sauce.
7. Taste and adjust seasoning with more salt and pepper if needed.
8. Remove the skillet from heat and transfer the sautéed shrimp and broccoli to a serving platter.
9. Serve hot, garnished with lemon wedges for squeezing over the shrimp and broccoli.
10. Enjoy your delicious and nutritious sautéed shrimp with garlic and broccoli as a flavorful main dish!

Quinoa Salad with Cucumber and Mint

Ingredients:

- 1 cup quinoa, rinsed
- 2 cups water or vegetable broth
- 1 cucumber, diced
- 1/4 cup red onion, finely chopped
- 1/4 cup fresh mint leaves, chopped
- 1/4 cup fresh parsley leaves, chopped
- 1/4 cup crumbled feta cheese (optional)
- 2 tablespoons olive oil
- 2 tablespoons lemon juice
- Salt and pepper to taste

Instructions:

1. In a medium saucepan, combine the quinoa and water or vegetable broth. Bring to a boil over medium-high heat.
2. Reduce the heat to low, cover, and simmer for 15-20 minutes, or until the quinoa is cooked and the liquid is absorbed. Remove from heat and let it sit covered for 5 minutes.
3. Fluff the cooked quinoa with a fork and transfer it to a large mixing bowl. Let it cool to room temperature.
4. Once the quinoa has cooled, add the diced cucumber, finely chopped red onion, chopped fresh mint leaves, chopped fresh parsley leaves, and crumbled feta cheese (if using) to the bowl.
5. In a small bowl, whisk together the olive oil and lemon juice. Pour the dressing over the quinoa salad.
6. Toss the salad until all ingredients are well combined and evenly coated with the dressing.
7. Taste and adjust seasoning with salt and pepper if needed.
8. Serve the quinoa salad immediately, or refrigerate for at least 30 minutes to allow the flavors to meld together before serving.
9. Enjoy your refreshing and flavorful quinoa salad with cucumber and mint as a side dish or light meal!

Eggplant Parmesan with Marinara Sauce

Ingredients:

For the Eggplant Parmesan:

- 2 medium eggplants, sliced into 1/2-inch rounds
- Salt
- 2 cups breadcrumbs (Italian seasoned breadcrumbs work well)
- 1 cup grated Parmesan cheese
- 2 large eggs, beaten
- Olive oil, for frying
- 2 cups marinara sauce (store-bought or homemade)
- 2 cups shredded mozzarella cheese

For the Marinara Sauce:

- 2 tablespoons olive oil
- 1 onion, finely chopped
- 2 cloves garlic, minced
- 1 can (28 ounces) crushed tomatoes
- 1 teaspoon dried oregano
- 1 teaspoon dried basil
- Salt and pepper to taste

Instructions:

1. Start by preparing the marinara sauce. In a large saucepan, heat the olive oil over medium heat. Add the chopped onion and cook until softened, about 5 minutes.
2. Add the minced garlic to the saucepan and cook for an additional minute until fragrant.
3. Stir in the crushed tomatoes, dried oregano, dried basil, salt, and pepper. Bring the sauce to a simmer and let it cook for about 20-25 minutes, stirring occasionally, until thickened. Taste and adjust seasoning as needed. Remove from heat and set aside.

4. While the marinara sauce is simmering, prepare the eggplant. Place the sliced eggplant rounds on a baking sheet and sprinkle both sides with salt. Let them sit for about 15-20 minutes to draw out excess moisture.
5. Preheat your oven to 375°F (190°C). Line a baking sheet with parchment paper.
6. In a shallow dish, combine the breadcrumbs and grated Parmesan cheese. In another shallow dish, place the beaten eggs.
7. Pat the eggplant slices dry with paper towels to remove the excess moisture. Dip each slice into the beaten eggs, then coat with the breadcrumb mixture, pressing gently to adhere.
8. Heat a generous amount of olive oil in a large skillet over medium heat. Working in batches, fry the breaded eggplant slices for 2-3 minutes on each side, or until golden brown and crispy. Add more oil to the skillet as needed for subsequent batches. Transfer the fried eggplant slices to a plate lined with paper towels to drain.
9. Once all the eggplant slices are fried, spread a thin layer of marinara sauce on the bottom of a baking dish. Place a layer of fried eggplant slices on top of the sauce.
10. Spoon more marinara sauce over the eggplant slices, then sprinkle shredded mozzarella cheese on top.
11. Repeat the layers with the remaining eggplant slices, marinara sauce, and mozzarella cheese, ending with a final layer of mozzarella cheese on top.
12. Cover the baking dish with aluminum foil and bake in the preheated oven for 25-30 minutes.
13. Remove the foil and bake for an additional 10-15 minutes, or until the cheese is melted and bubbly and the edges are golden brown.
14. Remove from the oven and let the Eggplant Parmesan rest for a few minutes before serving.
15. Serve hot, garnished with fresh basil or parsley if desired.
16. Enjoy your delicious Eggplant Parmesan with marinara sauce as a comforting and satisfying meal!

Mexican Cauliflower Rice Bowl

Ingredients:

For the Cauliflower Rice:

- 1 large head cauliflower, riced (about 4 cups)
- 1 tablespoon olive oil
- 1/2 onion, finely chopped
- 2 cloves garlic, minced
- 1 bell pepper, diced
- 1 teaspoon ground cumin
- 1 teaspoon chili powder
- Salt and pepper to taste
- 1/4 cup chopped fresh cilantro

For the Black Beans:

- 1 can (15 ounces) black beans, drained and rinsed
- 1/2 teaspoon ground cumin
- 1/2 teaspoon chili powder
- Salt to taste

For the Avocado Salsa:

- 2 ripe avocados, diced
- 1 tomato, diced
- 1/4 cup red onion, finely chopped
- 1/4 cup chopped fresh cilantro
- 1 tablespoon lime juice
- Salt and pepper to taste

Optional Toppings:

- Sliced jalapeños
- Shredded lettuce
- Sour cream or Greek yogurt

- Sliced radishes
- Lime wedges

Instructions:

1. Heat olive oil in a large skillet over medium heat. Add the chopped onion and cook until softened, about 5 minutes.
2. Add minced garlic and diced bell pepper to the skillet. Cook for an additional 2-3 minutes until the bell pepper is tender.
3. Stir in the ground cumin and chili powder, and cook for another minute until fragrant.
4. Add the riced cauliflower to the skillet and season with salt and pepper to taste. Cook, stirring occasionally, for 5-7 minutes, or until the cauliflower is tender.
5. While the cauliflower rice is cooking, prepare the black beans. In a small saucepan, combine the black beans, ground cumin, chili powder, and a pinch of salt. Heat over medium heat until warmed through. Keep warm until ready to serve.
6. To make the avocado salsa, combine diced avocados, diced tomato, chopped red onion, chopped cilantro, lime juice, salt, and pepper in a bowl. Gently toss to combine.
7. Once the cauliflower rice is cooked, stir in the chopped fresh cilantro.
8. To assemble the bowls, divide the cauliflower rice among serving bowls. Top each bowl with a portion of black beans and avocado salsa.
9. Add any desired optional toppings, such as sliced jalapeños, shredded lettuce, sour cream or Greek yogurt, sliced radishes, and lime wedges.
10. Serve immediately and enjoy your flavorful and nutritious Mexican Cauliflower Rice Bowl!

Baked Cod with Lemon and Herbs

Ingredients:

- 4 cod fillets (about 6 ounces each)
- Salt and pepper to taste
- 2 tablespoons olive oil
- 2 tablespoons fresh lemon juice
- 2 cloves garlic, minced
- 2 tablespoons chopped fresh parsley
- 1 tablespoon chopped fresh dill (or 1 teaspoon dried dill)
- 1 teaspoon chopped fresh thyme (or 1/2 teaspoon dried thyme)
- 1 lemon, thinly sliced
- Optional: lemon wedges for serving

Instructions:

1. Preheat your oven to 400°F (200°C). Lightly grease a baking dish with olive oil or non-stick cooking spray.
2. Pat the cod fillets dry with paper towels and place them in the prepared baking dish. Season both sides of the cod fillets with salt and pepper to taste.
3. In a small bowl, whisk together the olive oil, fresh lemon juice, minced garlic, chopped fresh parsley, chopped fresh dill, and chopped fresh thyme.
4. Drizzle the lemon and herb mixture over the cod fillets, making sure they are evenly coated.
5. Arrange the thinly sliced lemon rounds on top of the cod fillets.
6. Bake the cod in the preheated oven for 12-15 minutes, or until the fish is opaque and flakes easily with a fork.
7. If desired, broil the cod for an additional 1-2 minutes at the end to lightly brown the top.
8. Remove the baked cod from the oven and let it rest for a few minutes before serving.
9. Serve the baked cod with lemon and herbs hot, garnished with additional chopped fresh parsley or dill, and lemon wedges on the side for squeezing over the fish.
10. Enjoy your flavorful and tender baked cod with lemon and herbs as a delicious and healthy main dish!

Chickpea Salad with Cucumber and Red Onion

Ingredients:

- 2 cans (15 ounces each) chickpeas (garbanzo beans), drained and rinsed
- 1 English cucumber, diced
- 1/2 red onion, thinly sliced
- 1/4 cup chopped fresh parsley
- 2 tablespoons chopped fresh mint (optional)
- Juice of 1 lemon
- 2 tablespoons extra virgin olive oil
- Salt and pepper to taste

Instructions:

1. In a large mixing bowl, combine the drained and rinsed chickpeas, diced cucumber, thinly sliced red onion, chopped fresh parsley, and chopped fresh mint (if using).
2. In a small bowl, whisk together the lemon juice and extra virgin olive oil to make the dressing.
3. Pour the dressing over the chickpea salad and toss until well combined.
4. Season the salad with salt and pepper to taste, adjusting as needed.
5. Let the chickpea salad marinate in the refrigerator for at least 30 minutes to allow the flavors to meld together.
6. Before serving, give the salad a final toss to redistribute the dressing.
7. Serve the chickpea salad with cucumber and red onion as a side dish or light meal.
8. Enjoy its refreshing flavors and nutritious ingredients!

Turkey and Vegetable Stir-Fry

Ingredients:

- 1 lb turkey breast or turkey tenderloin, thinly sliced
- 2 tablespoons soy sauce
- 1 tablespoon oyster sauce
- 1 tablespoon hoisin sauce
- 1 tablespoon cornstarch
- 2 tablespoons vegetable oil, divided
- 2 cloves garlic, minced
- 1 tablespoon grated ginger
- 1 onion, thinly sliced
- 2 bell peppers (any color), thinly sliced
- 1 cup broccoli florets
- 1 carrot, thinly sliced
- Salt and pepper to taste
- Cooked rice or noodles, for serving
- Optional garnish: sliced green onions, sesame seeds

Instructions:

1. In a bowl, combine the sliced turkey with soy sauce, oyster sauce, hoisin sauce, and cornstarch. Mix well and let it marinate for at least 15 minutes.
2. Heat 1 tablespoon of vegetable oil in a large skillet or wok over medium-high heat. Add the marinated turkey slices and stir-fry for 2-3 minutes until browned and cooked through. Remove the turkey from the skillet and set aside.
3. In the same skillet, add the remaining tablespoon of vegetable oil. Add the minced garlic and grated ginger, and sauté for about 1 minute until fragrant.
4. Add the sliced onion, bell peppers, broccoli florets, and sliced carrot to the skillet. Stir-fry for 3-4 minutes until the vegetables are crisp-tender.
5. Return the cooked turkey to the skillet and toss everything together until well combined. Cook for another minute to heat through.
6. Season the stir-fry with salt and pepper to taste, adjusting as needed.
7. Serve the turkey and vegetable stir-fry hot over cooked rice or noodles.
8. Garnish with sliced green onions and sesame seeds, if desired.

9. Enjoy your flavorful and nutritious turkey and vegetable stir-fry as a delicious meal!

Caprese Salad with Balsamic Glaze

Ingredients:

- 2 large ripe tomatoes, sliced
- 1 ball fresh mozzarella cheese, sliced
- Fresh basil leaves
- Salt and pepper to taste
- Balsamic glaze (store-bought or homemade)

Instructions:

1. Arrange the tomato slices and fresh mozzarella slices alternately on a serving platter.
2. Tuck fresh basil leaves between the tomato and mozzarella slices.
3. Season the salad with salt and pepper to taste.
4. Drizzle balsamic glaze over the tomato, mozzarella, and basil.
5. Serve immediately as a refreshing appetizer or side dish.
6. Enjoy the classic combination of flavors in this Caprese salad with balsamic glaze!

Stuffed Portobello Mushrooms with Spinach and Goat Cheese

Ingredients:

- 4 large Portobello mushrooms
- 2 tablespoons olive oil
- 2 cloves garlic, minced
- 2 cups fresh spinach leaves, chopped
- 4 ounces goat cheese, crumbled
- Salt and pepper to taste
- 1/4 cup grated Parmesan cheese (optional, for topping)
- Fresh parsley or basil leaves for garnish (optional)

Instructions:

1. Preheat your oven to 375°F (190°C). Line a baking sheet with parchment paper or lightly grease it with olive oil.
2. Clean the Portobello mushrooms and remove the stems. Use a spoon to gently scrape out the gills from the inside of the mushrooms.
3. In a skillet, heat the olive oil over medium heat. Add the minced garlic and cook for 1 minute until fragrant.
4. Add the chopped spinach to the skillet and cook for 2-3 minutes until wilted. Season with salt and pepper to taste.
5. Remove the skillet from heat and let the spinach mixture cool slightly.
6. Once cooled, stir in the crumbled goat cheese until well combined.
7. Stuff each Portobello mushroom with the spinach and goat cheese mixture, pressing down gently to compact the filling.
8. Place the stuffed mushrooms on the prepared baking sheet.
9. Optionally, sprinkle grated Parmesan cheese over the stuffed mushrooms for an extra cheesy topping.
10. Bake in the preheated oven for 15-20 minutes, or until the mushrooms are tender and the filling is heated through and slightly browned on top.
11. Remove the stuffed Portobello mushrooms from the oven and let them cool for a few minutes before serving.
12. Garnish with fresh parsley or basil leaves, if desired, before serving.
13. Enjoy your delicious stuffed Portobello mushrooms with spinach and goat cheese as a flavorful appetizer or vegetarian main dish!

Chicken Lettuce Cups with Asian Sauce

Ingredients:

For the Chicken Filling:

- 1 lb ground chicken
- 2 tablespoons vegetable oil
- 2 cloves garlic, minced
- 1 tablespoon ginger, minced
- 1/4 cup soy sauce
- 2 tablespoons hoisin sauce
- 1 tablespoon rice vinegar
- 1 tablespoon sesame oil
- 1 teaspoon sriracha sauce (adjust to taste)
- 1 cup water chestnuts, chopped
- 1/4 cup green onions, chopped
- Salt and pepper to taste

For Serving:

- 1 head butter lettuce or iceberg lettuce, leaves separated and washed
- Optional toppings: chopped peanuts, sliced red chili, chopped cilantro, lime wedges

Instructions:

1. Heat vegetable oil in a large skillet or wok over medium heat. Add minced garlic and ginger, and sauté for about 1 minute until fragrant.
2. Add ground chicken to the skillet and cook, breaking it apart with a spoon, until it is no longer pink.
3. In a small bowl, whisk together soy sauce, hoisin sauce, rice vinegar, sesame oil, and sriracha sauce.
4. Pour the sauce mixture over the cooked chicken in the skillet and stir to combine.
5. Add chopped water chestnuts and green onions to the skillet, and continue to cook for another 2-3 minutes until heated through.
6. Season with salt and pepper to taste, and adjust the seasoning if needed.

7. To serve, spoon the chicken mixture into lettuce leaves to create cups.
8. Optional: Garnish with chopped peanuts, sliced red chili, chopped cilantro, and serve with lime wedges on the side.
9. Enjoy your delicious and flavorful chicken lettuce cups with Asian sauce as a light and satisfying meal or appetizer!

Ratatouille with Quinoa

Ingredients:

For the Ratatouille:

- 1 eggplant, diced
- 2 zucchinis, diced
- 1 bell pepper, diced
- 1 onion, diced
- 2 cloves garlic, minced
- 2 cups diced tomatoes (fresh or canned)
- 2 tablespoons tomato paste
- 1 teaspoon dried thyme
- 1 teaspoon dried oregano
- Salt and pepper to taste
- 2 tablespoons olive oil
- Fresh basil leaves for garnish (optional)

For the Quinoa:

- 1 cup quinoa, rinsed
- 2 cups water or vegetable broth
- Salt to taste

Instructions:

1. Preheat your oven to 375°F (190°C).
2. In a large skillet or Dutch oven, heat olive oil over medium heat. Add diced onion and minced garlic, and sauté until softened and fragrant.
3. Add diced eggplant, zucchini, and bell pepper to the skillet. Cook for about 5 minutes, stirring occasionally, until the vegetables begin to soften.
4. Stir in diced tomatoes, tomato paste, dried thyme, dried oregano, salt, and pepper. Mix well to combine.
5. Cover the skillet or Dutch oven and transfer it to the preheated oven. Bake for 25-30 minutes, or until the vegetables are tender and cooked through.

6. While the ratatouille is cooking, prepare the quinoa. In a saucepan, combine rinsed quinoa and water or vegetable broth. Bring to a boil, then reduce heat to low, cover, and simmer for 15-20 minutes, or until the quinoa is cooked and the liquid is absorbed. Fluff with a fork and season with salt to taste.
7. Once the ratatouille is done, remove it from the oven and let it cool slightly.
8. To serve, spoon the ratatouille over cooked quinoa in individual bowls.
9. Garnish with fresh basil leaves, if desired.
10. Enjoy your delicious ratatouille with quinoa as a flavorful and nutritious meal!

Greek Yogurt Chicken Salad with Grapes and Walnuts

Ingredients:

- 2 cups cooked chicken breast, diced or shredded
- 1 cup seedless grapes, halved
- 1/2 cup chopped walnuts
- 1/4 cup diced celery
- 1/4 cup diced red onion
- 1/2 cup plain Greek yogurt
- 1 tablespoon lemon juice
- 1 tablespoon honey
- 1 teaspoon Dijon mustard
- Salt and pepper to taste
- Lettuce leaves or bread for serving (optional)

Instructions:

1. In a large mixing bowl, combine the cooked chicken breast, halved grapes, chopped walnuts, diced celery, and diced red onion.
2. In a small bowl, whisk together the plain Greek yogurt, lemon juice, honey, Dijon mustard, salt, and pepper until smooth and well combined.
3. Pour the yogurt dressing over the chicken salad mixture.
4. Gently toss everything together until the chicken and other ingredients are evenly coated with the dressing.
5. Taste and adjust seasoning with more salt and pepper if needed.
6. Cover the bowl and refrigerate the chicken salad for at least 30 minutes to allow the flavors to meld together.
7. Once chilled, serve the Greek yogurt chicken salad on a bed of lettuce leaves or with bread slices, if desired.
8. Enjoy your creamy and flavorful chicken salad with grapes and walnuts as a light and satisfying meal or sandwich filling!

Veggie Frittata with Sweet Potato Crust

Ingredients:

For the Sweet Potato Crust:

- 2 medium sweet potatoes, peeled and thinly sliced
- 2 tablespoons olive oil
- Salt and pepper to taste

For the Frittata:

- 8 large eggs
- 1/4 cup milk or unsweetened almond milk
- 1 cup chopped vegetables of your choice (bell peppers, spinach, onions, mushrooms, tomatoes, etc.)
- 1/2 cup shredded cheese (cheddar, mozzarella, feta, etc.)
- Salt and pepper to taste
- Fresh herbs for garnish (optional)

Instructions:

1. Preheat your oven to 375°F (190°C). Lightly grease a 9-inch pie dish or baking pan.
2. Arrange the thinly sliced sweet potatoes in the bottom of the prepared pie dish, overlapping them slightly to form a crust. Drizzle with olive oil and season with salt and pepper.
3. Bake the sweet potato crust in the preheated oven for 15-20 minutes, or until the sweet potatoes are tender and slightly golden around the edges.
4. While the crust is baking, prepare the frittata filling. In a large mixing bowl, whisk together the eggs and milk until well combined. Season with salt and pepper to taste.
5. Stir in the chopped vegetables and shredded cheese into the egg mixture.
6. Once the sweet potato crust is done baking, remove it from the oven and pour the egg mixture over the top, spreading it out evenly.

7. Return the frittata to the oven and bake for an additional 20-25 minutes, or until the eggs are set and the top is golden brown.
8. Once cooked through, remove the frittata from the oven and let it cool for a few minutes before slicing.
9. Garnish with fresh herbs, if desired, before serving.
10. Slice and serve the veggie frittata with sweet potato crust warm or at room temperature.
11. Enjoy this delicious and nutritious meal for breakfast, brunch, or any time of the day!

Shrimp and Avocado Salad with Lime Dressing

Ingredients:

For the Salad:

- 1 lb large shrimp, peeled and deveined
- 2 avocados, diced
- 1 cup cherry tomatoes, halved
- 1/4 cup red onion, thinly sliced
- 1/4 cup chopped fresh cilantro
- Salt and pepper to taste
- Optional: mixed salad greens for serving

For the Lime Dressing:

- 3 tablespoons olive oil
- 2 tablespoons fresh lime juice
- 1 clove garlic, minced
- 1 teaspoon honey or maple syrup
- 1/2 teaspoon ground cumin
- Salt and pepper to taste

Instructions:

1. In a large mixing bowl, combine the diced avocados, halved cherry tomatoes, thinly sliced red onion, and chopped fresh cilantro. If using mixed salad greens, add them to the bowl as well.
2. Season the salad with salt and pepper to taste, and toss gently to combine.
3. In a small bowl, whisk together the olive oil, fresh lime juice, minced garlic, honey or maple syrup, ground cumin, salt, and pepper to make the lime dressing.
4. Pour the lime dressing over the shrimp and avocado salad, and toss gently to coat everything evenly.
5. Heat a skillet over medium-high heat. Add a drizzle of olive oil to the skillet.
6. Add the peeled and deveined shrimp to the skillet and cook for 2-3 minutes per side, or until pink and opaque.
7. Once cooked, transfer the shrimp to the salad bowl.

8. Gently toss the salad again to incorporate the cooked shrimp.
9. Serve the shrimp and avocado salad with lime dressing immediately, garnished with additional cilantro if desired.
10. Enjoy this refreshing and flavorful salad as a light and satisfying meal!

Lentil and Vegetable Curry

Ingredients:

- 1 cup dried lentils (brown or green), rinsed
- 3 cups vegetable broth or water
- 2 tablespoons olive oil
- 1 onion, chopped
- 3 cloves garlic, minced
- 1 tablespoon fresh ginger, minced
- 1 bell pepper, diced
- 2 carrots, diced
- 1 zucchini, diced
- 1 cup cauliflower florets
- 1 cup canned diced tomatoes
- 1 can (14 ounces) coconut milk
- 2 tablespoons curry powder
- 1 teaspoon ground cumin
- 1 teaspoon ground coriander
- 1/2 teaspoon turmeric powder
- Salt and pepper to taste
- Fresh cilantro leaves for garnish (optional)
- Cooked rice or naan bread for serving

Instructions:

1. In a large pot, combine the rinsed lentils and vegetable broth or water. Bring to a boil, then reduce heat to low, cover, and simmer for about 20-25 minutes, or until the lentils are tender. Drain any excess liquid and set aside.
2. In a separate large skillet or saucepan, heat the olive oil over medium heat. Add the chopped onion, minced garlic, and minced ginger, and sauté for 2-3 minutes until fragrant.
3. Add the diced bell pepper, carrots, zucchini, and cauliflower florets to the skillet. Cook for 5-7 minutes, stirring occasionally, until the vegetables are slightly softened.
4. Stir in the canned diced tomatoes, coconut milk, curry powder, ground cumin, ground coriander, turmeric powder, salt, and pepper. Mix well to combine.

5. Bring the mixture to a simmer, then reduce heat to low and let it cook for about 10-15 minutes, allowing the flavors to meld together and the vegetables to become tender.
6. Once the vegetables are cooked to your desired tenderness, add the cooked lentils to the skillet and stir to combine. Cook for an additional 5 minutes to heat through.
7. Taste and adjust seasoning with more salt and pepper if needed.
8. Serve the lentil and vegetable curry hot, garnished with fresh cilantro leaves if desired.
9. Enjoy your delicious and hearty lentil and vegetable curry with cooked rice or naan bread on the side!

Turkey and Quinoa Stuffed Bell Peppers

Ingredients:

- 4 large bell peppers (any color), tops removed and seeds removed
- 1 tablespoon olive oil
- 1 onion, diced
- 2 cloves garlic, minced
- 1 lb ground turkey
- 1 cup cooked quinoa
- 1 can (14.5 ounces) diced tomatoes, drained
- 1 teaspoon dried oregano
- 1 teaspoon dried basil
- Salt and pepper to taste
- 1 cup shredded cheese (cheddar, mozzarella, etc.), divided
- Fresh parsley or basil leaves for garnish (optional)

Instructions:

1. Preheat your oven to 375°F (190°C). Grease a baking dish large enough to hold the bell peppers upright.
2. In a large skillet, heat olive oil over medium heat. Add diced onion and minced garlic, and sauté until softened and fragrant, about 3-4 minutes.
3. Add ground turkey to the skillet and cook until browned and cooked through, breaking it apart with a spoon as it cooks.
4. Stir in cooked quinoa, drained diced tomatoes, dried oregano, dried basil, salt, and pepper. Cook for an additional 2-3 minutes until heated through and well combined.
5. Remove the skillet from heat and stir in 1/2 cup of shredded cheese until melted and incorporated into the mixture.
6. Stuff each bell pepper with the turkey and quinoa mixture, pressing down gently to fill completely.
7. Place the stuffed bell peppers upright in the prepared baking dish.
8. Sprinkle the remaining 1/2 cup of shredded cheese evenly over the tops of the stuffed bell peppers.
9. Cover the baking dish with aluminum foil and bake in the preheated oven for 25-30 minutes.

10. Remove the foil and bake for an additional 10-15 minutes, or until the bell peppers are tender and the cheese is melted and bubbly.
11. Remove the stuffed bell peppers from the oven and let them cool for a few minutes before serving.
12. Garnish with fresh parsley or basil leaves, if desired, before serving.
13. Enjoy your delicious and nutritious turkey and quinoa stuffed bell peppers as a satisfying meal!

Spaghetti Squash with Turkey Meatballs

Ingredients:

For the Turkey Meatballs:

- 1 lb ground turkey
- 1/2 cup breadcrumbs (or almond meal for a gluten-free option)
- 1/4 cup grated Parmesan cheese
- 1 egg
- 2 cloves garlic, minced
- 2 tablespoons chopped fresh parsley
- 1 teaspoon dried oregano
- Salt and pepper to taste
- Olive oil for cooking

For the Spaghetti Squash:

- 1 medium spaghetti squash
- Olive oil
- Salt and pepper to taste

For the Sauce:

- 2 cups marinara sauce (store-bought or homemade)
- Fresh basil leaves for garnish (optional)

Instructions:

1. Preheat your oven to 400°F (200°C).
2. Cut the spaghetti squash in half lengthwise and scoop out the seeds and membranes with a spoon.
3. Drizzle the cut sides of the spaghetti squash with olive oil and season with salt and pepper. Place the halves, cut side down, on a baking sheet lined with parchment paper.

4. Roast the spaghetti squash in the preheated oven for 35-45 minutes, or until the flesh is tender and easily pierced with a fork. Remove from the oven and let it cool slightly.
5. While the spaghetti squash is roasting, prepare the turkey meatballs. In a large mixing bowl, combine ground turkey, breadcrumbs, grated Parmesan cheese, egg, minced garlic, chopped fresh parsley, dried oregano, salt, and pepper. Mix until well combined.
6. Shape the turkey mixture into meatballs, about 1 to 1.5 inches in diameter.
7. Heat olive oil in a large skillet over medium heat. Add the turkey meatballs to the skillet and cook, turning occasionally, until browned on all sides and cooked through, about 10-12 minutes. Remove from heat and set aside.
8. Once the spaghetti squash is done roasting, use a fork to scrape the flesh into strands. Transfer the spaghetti squash strands to a serving platter or individual plates.
9. Heat the marinara sauce in a saucepan over medium heat until warmed through.
10. Top the spaghetti squash strands with the warm marinara sauce and turkey meatballs.
11. Garnish with fresh basil leaves, if desired, before serving.
12. Serve hot and enjoy your delicious spaghetti squash with turkey meatballs as a healthy and satisfying meal!

Greek Lemon Chicken Soup

Ingredients:

- 6 cups chicken broth
- 1/2 cup uncooked white rice
- 2 boneless, skinless chicken breasts
- 3 large eggs
- 1/3 cup fresh lemon juice
- Zest of 1 lemon
- Salt and pepper to taste
- Chopped fresh dill or parsley for garnish (optional)

Instructions:

1. In a large pot, bring the chicken broth to a boil over medium-high heat.
2. Add the uncooked rice to the boiling broth and reduce the heat to low. Simmer for about 15 minutes, or until the rice is cooked and tender.
3. While the rice is cooking, cut the chicken breasts into small, bite-sized pieces.
4. Once the rice is cooked, add the diced chicken to the pot and simmer for an additional 10-12 minutes, or until the chicken is cooked through.
5. In a mixing bowl, whisk together the eggs, lemon juice, and lemon zest until well combined.
6. Gradually add a ladleful of the hot broth from the pot into the egg mixture, whisking constantly to temper the eggs.
7. Slowly pour the tempered egg mixture back into the pot, stirring continuously.
8. Continue to cook the soup over low heat for another 5 minutes, stirring occasionally, until the soup thickens slightly.
9. Season the soup with salt and pepper to taste, adjusting as needed.
10. Remove the soup from heat and let it cool slightly before serving.
11. Ladle the Greek lemon chicken soup into bowls and garnish with chopped fresh dill or parsley, if desired.
12. Serve hot and enjoy this comforting and flavorful Avgolemono Soup!

Cauliflower Fried Rice with Chicken and Vegetables

Ingredients:

- 1 medium head cauliflower
- 2 tablespoons olive oil
- 2 boneless, skinless chicken breasts, diced
- Salt and pepper to taste
- 2 eggs, beaten
- 1 onion, diced
- 2 cloves garlic, minced
- 1 cup mixed vegetables (such as diced carrots, peas, bell peppers, and/or corn)
- 3 tablespoons soy sauce (or tamari for gluten-free option)
- 1 tablespoon sesame oil
- 2 green onions, chopped (for garnish)
- Sesame seeds (for garnish)

Instructions:

1. Cut the cauliflower into florets and place them in a food processor. Pulse until the cauliflower resembles rice-like grains.
2. Heat 1 tablespoon of olive oil in a large skillet or wok over medium-high heat. Add the diced chicken breasts, season with salt and pepper, and cook until browned and cooked through. Remove the chicken from the skillet and set aside.
3. In the same skillet, add the beaten eggs and cook, stirring occasionally, until scrambled. Remove the scrambled eggs from the skillet and set aside.
4. Heat the remaining tablespoon of olive oil in the skillet. Add the diced onion and minced garlic, and sauté until softened and fragrant.
5. Add the mixed vegetables to the skillet and cook until tender, about 3-5 minutes.
6. Stir in the riced cauliflower and cook for an additional 5-7 minutes, stirring frequently, until the cauliflower is tender.
7. Return the cooked chicken and scrambled eggs to the skillet with the cauliflower and vegetables.
8. Drizzle the soy sauce and sesame oil over the mixture, and toss everything together until well combined and heated through.
9. Taste and adjust seasoning with more salt and pepper if needed.
10. Remove the cauliflower fried rice from heat and transfer to serving plates.
11. Garnish with chopped green onions and sesame seeds before serving.

12. Enjoy your flavorful and nutritious cauliflower fried rice with chicken and vegetables!

Black Bean and Corn Salad with Cilantro Lime Dressing

Ingredients:

For the Salad:

- 1 can (15 ounces) black beans, drained and rinsed
- 1 cup corn kernels (fresh, canned, or frozen)
- 1 red bell pepper, diced
- 1/2 red onion, finely chopped
- 1 jalapeño pepper, seeded and diced (optional for heat)
- 1/4 cup chopped fresh cilantro leaves
- Salt and pepper to taste
- Optional: diced avocado for serving

For the Cilantro Lime Dressing:

- 1/4 cup fresh lime juice (about 2-3 limes)
- 2 tablespoons olive oil
- 1 tablespoon honey or maple syrup
- 2 cloves garlic, minced
- 1/4 cup chopped fresh cilantro leaves
- Salt and pepper to taste

Instructions:

1. In a large mixing bowl, combine the black beans, corn kernels, diced red bell pepper, finely chopped red onion, diced jalapeño pepper (if using), and chopped fresh cilantro leaves.
2. Season the salad with salt and pepper to taste, and toss gently to combine.
3. In a small bowl, whisk together the fresh lime juice, olive oil, honey or maple syrup, minced garlic, chopped fresh cilantro leaves, salt, and pepper to make the cilantro lime dressing.
4. Pour the cilantro lime dressing over the black bean and corn salad, and toss until everything is well coated with the dressing.
5. Cover the bowl and refrigerate the salad for at least 30 minutes to allow the flavors to meld together.

6. Before serving, give the salad a final toss to redistribute the dressing.
7. If desired, serve the black bean and corn salad with diced avocado on top.
8. Enjoy your refreshing and flavorful black bean and corn salad with cilantro lime dressing as a side dish or light meal!

Grilled Salmon with Asparagus and Lemon Dill Sauce

Ingredients:

For the Grilled Salmon:

- 4 salmon fillets
- Salt and pepper to taste
- 2 tablespoons olive oil
- 2 cloves garlic, minced
- 1 lemon, sliced
- Fresh dill for garnish

For the Asparagus:

- 1 bunch asparagus, woody ends trimmed
- 1 tablespoon olive oil
- Salt and pepper to taste
- Lemon wedges for serving

For the Lemon Dill Sauce:

- 1/2 cup Greek yogurt
- 2 tablespoons fresh lemon juice
- 1 tablespoon chopped fresh dill
- 1 teaspoon Dijon mustard
- Salt and pepper to taste

Instructions:

1. Preheat your grill to medium-high heat.
2. Season the salmon fillets with salt and pepper to taste.
3. In a small bowl, mix together the olive oil and minced garlic. Brush the mixture over the salmon fillets.
4. Place the lemon slices on top of the salmon fillets.
5. Grill the salmon fillets for 4-5 minutes per side, or until cooked through and flaky. Cooking time will depend on the thickness of your salmon fillets.

6. While the salmon is grilling, toss the trimmed asparagus with olive oil, salt, and pepper.
7. Grill the asparagus alongside the salmon for about 3-4 minutes, or until tender and lightly charred.
8. In a small bowl, whisk together the Greek yogurt, fresh lemon juice, chopped fresh dill, Dijon mustard, salt, and pepper to make the lemon dill sauce.
9. Once the salmon and asparagus are done grilling, remove them from the grill and transfer to serving plates.
10. Drizzle the lemon dill sauce over the grilled salmon.
11. Garnish with fresh dill and serve with lemon wedges on the side.
12. Enjoy your delicious grilled salmon with asparagus and lemon dill sauce!

Mediterranean Chickpea Salad with Feta

Ingredients:

- 2 cans (15 ounces each) chickpeas (garbanzo beans), drained and rinsed
- 1 cucumber, diced
- 1 bell pepper (red, yellow, or orange), diced
- 1 pint cherry tomatoes, halved
- 1/2 red onion, thinly sliced
- 1/4 cup chopped fresh parsley
- 1/4 cup chopped fresh mint
- 4 ounces feta cheese, crumbled
- Salt and pepper to taste

For the Dressing:

- 1/4 cup extra virgin olive oil
- 2 tablespoons red wine vinegar
- 1 clove garlic, minced
- 1 teaspoon Dijon mustard
- 1 teaspoon honey or maple syrup
- 1/2 teaspoon dried oregano
- Salt and pepper to taste

Instructions:

1. In a large mixing bowl, combine the drained and rinsed chickpeas, diced cucumber, diced bell pepper, halved cherry tomatoes, thinly sliced red onion, chopped fresh parsley, and chopped fresh mint.
2. In a small bowl, whisk together the extra virgin olive oil, red wine vinegar, minced garlic, Dijon mustard, honey or maple syrup, dried oregano, salt, and pepper to make the dressing.
3. Pour the dressing over the chickpea salad and toss until everything is well coated.
4. Gently fold in the crumbled feta cheese.
5. Taste and adjust seasoning with more salt and pepper if needed.
6. Cover the bowl and refrigerate the chickpea salad for at least 30 minutes to allow the flavors to meld together.

7. Before serving, give the salad a final toss to redistribute the dressing.
8. Serve the Mediterranean chickpea salad with feta as a refreshing side dish or light meal.
9. Enjoy the vibrant flavors and textures of this delicious salad!

Tofu and Veggie Stir-Fry with Ginger Sauce

Ingredients:

For the Stir-Fry:

- 14 oz (400g) firm tofu, pressed and cubed
- 2 tablespoons soy sauce
- 2 tablespoons cornstarch
- 2 tablespoons sesame oil, divided
- 1 tablespoon vegetable oil
- 2 cups mixed vegetables (such as bell peppers, broccoli, carrots, snap peas, etc.), sliced or diced
- 3 cloves garlic, minced
- 1 tablespoon fresh ginger, minced
- Cooked rice or noodles for serving

For the Ginger Sauce:

- 1/4 cup soy sauce
- 2 tablespoons rice vinegar
- 2 tablespoons water
- 2 tablespoons honey or maple syrup
- 1 tablespoon cornstarch
- 1 tablespoon fresh ginger, grated
- 2 cloves garlic, minced
- Red pepper flakes to taste (optional)

Instructions:

1. In a shallow dish, combine the cubed tofu with 2 tablespoons of soy sauce and 2 tablespoons of cornstarch. Toss gently to coat the tofu evenly.
2. Heat 1 tablespoon of sesame oil and vegetable oil in a large skillet or wok over medium-high heat. Add the tofu cubes and cook until golden brown and crispy on all sides, about 5-7 minutes. Remove the tofu from the skillet and set aside.

3. In the same skillet, add the remaining tablespoon of sesame oil. Add the minced garlic and ginger, and sauté for about 1 minute until fragrant.
4. Add the mixed vegetables to the skillet and stir-fry for 4-5 minutes, or until they are tender-crisp.
5. While the vegetables are cooking, prepare the ginger sauce. In a small bowl, whisk together the soy sauce, rice vinegar, water, honey or maple syrup, cornstarch, grated ginger, minced garlic, and red pepper flakes (if using).
6. Pour the ginger sauce into the skillet with the cooked vegetables. Stir well to combine.
7. Return the cooked tofu to the skillet and toss everything together until the tofu and vegetables are coated with the sauce and heated through.
8. Taste and adjust seasoning if needed, adding more soy sauce or honey according to your preference.
9. Serve the tofu and veggie stir-fry hot over cooked rice or noodles.
10. Enjoy your flavorful and nutritious tofu and veggie stir-fry with ginger sauce!

Egg Salad Lettuce Wraps

Ingredients:

- 6 hard-boiled eggs, peeled and chopped
- 1/4 cup mayonnaise
- 1 tablespoon Dijon mustard
- 2 tablespoons finely chopped celery
- 2 tablespoons finely chopped red onion
- 1 tablespoon chopped fresh dill (optional)
- Salt and pepper to taste
- Lettuce leaves (such as butter lettuce, romaine, or iceberg) for wrapping
- Optional toppings: sliced cherry tomatoes, avocado slices, cucumber slices, sprouts, etc.

Instructions:

1. In a mixing bowl, combine the chopped hard-boiled eggs, mayonnaise, Dijon mustard, chopped celery, chopped red onion, and chopped fresh dill (if using).
2. Stir everything together until well combined and the ingredients are evenly distributed.
3. Season the egg salad with salt and pepper to taste, adjusting as needed.
4. Arrange the lettuce leaves on a serving platter or individual plates.
5. Spoon the egg salad mixture onto each lettuce leaf, dividing it evenly among them.
6. Optionally, top each lettuce wrap with sliced cherry tomatoes, avocado slices, cucumber slices, sprouts, or any other desired toppings.
7. Serve the egg salad lettuce wraps immediately, or cover and refrigerate until ready to serve.
8. Enjoy your light and satisfying egg salad lettuce wraps as a nutritious meal or snack!

Roasted Vegetable Quinoa Bowl

Ingredients:

For the Roasted Vegetables:

- 2 cups mixed vegetables (such as bell peppers, zucchini, cherry tomatoes, red onion, broccoli, cauliflower, etc.), chopped
- 2 tablespoons olive oil
- 2 cloves garlic, minced
- 1 teaspoon dried herbs (such as thyme, rosemary, or Italian seasoning)
- Salt and pepper to taste

For the Quinoa:

- 1 cup quinoa, rinsed
- 2 cups vegetable broth or water
- Salt to taste

For the Lemon Tahini Dressing:

- 1/4 cup tahini
- 2 tablespoons fresh lemon juice
- 2 tablespoons water
- 1 clove garlic, minced
- 1 teaspoon honey or maple syrup (optional)
- Salt and pepper to taste

Optional Toppings:

- Fresh herbs (such as parsley or cilantro), chopped
- Avocado slices
- Toasted nuts or seeds (such as almonds, pumpkin seeds, or sunflower seeds)
- Crumbled feta cheese or goat cheese

Instructions:

1. Preheat your oven to 400°F (200°C). Line a baking sheet with parchment paper or lightly grease it.
2. In a large mixing bowl, toss the chopped mixed vegetables with olive oil, minced garlic, dried herbs, salt, and pepper until evenly coated.
3. Spread the seasoned vegetables out in a single layer on the prepared baking sheet.
4. Roast the vegetables in the preheated oven for 20-25 minutes, or until they are tender and slightly caramelized, stirring halfway through cooking.
5. While the vegetables are roasting, prepare the quinoa. In a saucepan, combine the rinsed quinoa and vegetable broth or water. Bring to a boil, then reduce heat to low, cover, and simmer for 15-20 minutes, or until the quinoa is cooked and the liquid is absorbed. Fluff with a fork and season with salt to taste.
6. In a small bowl, whisk together the tahini, fresh lemon juice, water, minced garlic, honey or maple syrup (if using), salt, and pepper to make the lemon tahini dressing. Adjust consistency with more water if needed.
7. To assemble the bowls, divide the cooked quinoa among serving bowls. Top with the roasted vegetables.
8. Drizzle the lemon tahini dressing over the quinoa and roasted vegetables.
9. Garnish the bowls with chopped fresh herbs, avocado slices, toasted nuts or seeds, and crumbled feta cheese or goat cheese, if desired.
10. Serve the roasted vegetable quinoa bowls warm, and enjoy a flavorful and nutritious meal!

Turkey Chili with Butternut Squash

Ingredients:

- 1 tablespoon olive oil
- 1 onion, chopped
- 3 cloves garlic, minced
- 1 lb ground turkey
- 2 cups diced butternut squash
- 1 bell pepper, diced
- 1 can (14.5 oz) diced tomatoes
- 1 can (15 oz) black beans, drained and rinsed
- 1 can (15 oz) kidney beans, drained and rinsed
- 2 cups chicken or vegetable broth
- 2 tablespoons chili powder
- 1 teaspoon ground cumin
- 1 teaspoon paprika
- 1/2 teaspoon dried oregano
- Salt and pepper to taste
- Optional toppings: shredded cheese, chopped cilantro, sour cream, sliced green onions, avocado, etc.

Instructions:

1. Heat the olive oil in a large pot or Dutch oven over medium heat.
2. Add the chopped onion and minced garlic to the pot, and sauté until softened and fragrant, about 2-3 minutes.
3. Add the ground turkey to the pot, breaking it apart with a spoon, and cook until browned and cooked through.
4. Stir in the diced butternut squash and bell pepper, and cook for another 5 minutes, stirring occasionally.
5. Add the diced tomatoes (with their juices), black beans, kidney beans, chicken or vegetable broth, chili powder, ground cumin, paprika, dried oregano, salt, and pepper to the pot.
6. Stir well to combine all the ingredients.
7. Bring the chili to a boil, then reduce the heat to low and simmer, covered, for about 20-25 minutes, or until the butternut squash is tender and the flavors have melded together.

8. Taste and adjust seasoning with more salt and pepper if needed.
9. Serve the turkey chili with butternut squash hot, garnished with your choice of toppings such as shredded cheese, chopped cilantro, sour cream, sliced green onions, avocado, etc.
10. Enjoy your hearty and delicious turkey chili with butternut squash on a chilly day!

Baked Chicken with Brussels Sprouts and Bacon

Ingredients:

- 4 boneless, skinless chicken breasts
- Salt and pepper to taste
- 1 tablespoon olive oil
- 1 lb Brussels sprouts, trimmed and halved
- 4 slices bacon, chopped
- 2 cloves garlic, minced
- 1/2 teaspoon dried thyme
- 1/4 teaspoon red pepper flakes (optional)
- 1/4 cup chicken broth or water
- 2 tablespoons grated Parmesan cheese (optional)
- Fresh parsley for garnish (optional)

Instructions:

1. Preheat your oven to 400°F (200°C).
2. Season the chicken breasts with salt and pepper to taste.
3. Heat the olive oil in a large oven-safe skillet over medium-high heat.
4. Add the seasoned chicken breasts to the skillet and sear for 2-3 minutes on each side, until golden brown. Remove the chicken from the skillet and set aside.
5. In the same skillet, add the chopped bacon and cook until crispy.
6. Add the halved Brussels sprouts to the skillet with the bacon and cook for about 5 minutes, stirring occasionally, until they begin to brown.
7. Stir in the minced garlic, dried thyme, and red pepper flakes (if using), and cook for another minute until fragrant.
8. Pour the chicken broth or water into the skillet and stir, scraping up any browned bits from the bottom of the pan.
9. Return the seared chicken breasts to the skillet, nestling them among the Brussels sprouts and bacon.
10. Transfer the skillet to the preheated oven and bake for 20-25 minutes, or until the chicken is cooked through and the Brussels sprouts are tender.
11. If desired, sprinkle grated Parmesan cheese over the chicken and Brussels sprouts during the last few minutes of baking.
12. Remove the skillet from the oven and let it rest for a few minutes.
13. Garnish with fresh parsley before serving, if desired.

14. Serve the baked chicken with Brussels sprouts and bacon hot, and enjoy your flavorful and comforting meal!

Greek Quinoa Stuffed Peppers

Ingredients:

- 4 large bell peppers (any color), halved and seeds removed
- 1 cup quinoa, rinsed
- 2 cups vegetable broth or water
- 1 tablespoon olive oil
- 1 small onion, diced
- 2 cloves garlic, minced
- 1 cup cherry tomatoes, halved
- 1/2 cup Kalamata olives, pitted and chopped
- 1/2 cup crumbled feta cheese
- 1/4 cup chopped fresh parsley
- 1 tablespoon lemon juice
- 1 teaspoon dried oregano
- Salt and pepper to taste
- Optional: extra feta cheese and parsley for garnish

Instructions:

1. Preheat your oven to 375°F (190°C). Grease a baking dish large enough to hold the halved bell peppers.
2. In a saucepan, combine the quinoa and vegetable broth or water. Bring to a boil, then reduce heat to low, cover, and simmer for 15-20 minutes, or until the quinoa is cooked and the liquid is absorbed. Remove from heat and fluff with a fork.
3. While the quinoa is cooking, heat olive oil in a skillet over medium heat. Add diced onion and minced garlic, and sauté until softened and fragrant.
4. Add halved cherry tomatoes to the skillet and cook for 3-4 minutes, until they begin to soften.
5. In a large mixing bowl, combine the cooked quinoa, sautéed onion and garlic, cherry tomatoes, chopped Kalamata olives, crumbled feta cheese, chopped fresh parsley, lemon juice, dried oregano, salt, and pepper. Mix well to combine.
6. Place the halved bell peppers in the prepared baking dish, cut side up.
7. Spoon the quinoa mixture evenly into each bell pepper half, pressing gently to pack it in.

8. Cover the baking dish with aluminum foil and bake in the preheated oven for 25-30 minutes, or until the peppers are tender.
9. Remove the foil and optionally sprinkle extra crumbled feta cheese and chopped parsley over the stuffed peppers.
10. Return the baking dish to the oven and bake, uncovered, for an additional 5 minutes, or until the cheese is melted and bubbly.
11. Remove the stuffed peppers from the oven and let them cool for a few minutes before serving.
12. Serve the Greek quinoa stuffed peppers hot, and enjoy this flavorful and nutritious dish!

Spinach and Mushroom Omelette

Ingredients:

- 3 large eggs
- 1 tablespoon milk (optional)
- Salt and pepper to taste
- 1 tablespoon olive oil or butter
- 1 cup sliced mushrooms
- 1 cup fresh spinach leaves, washed and chopped
- 1/4 cup shredded cheese (such as cheddar, mozzarella, or feta) (optional)
- Optional additions: diced onions, minced garlic, diced tomatoes, chopped bell peppers, etc.

Instructions:

1. In a small bowl, whisk together the eggs and milk (if using) until well combined. Season with salt and pepper to taste.
2. Heat olive oil or butter in a non-stick skillet over medium heat.
3. Add the sliced mushrooms to the skillet and cook for 3-4 minutes, stirring occasionally, until they begin to soften.
4. Add the chopped spinach to the skillet and cook for another 1-2 minutes, until wilted.
5. If using any additional ingredients like onions, garlic, tomatoes, or bell peppers, add them to the skillet and cook for a few minutes until softened.
6. Pour the whisked eggs evenly over the cooked vegetables in the skillet.
7. Allow the eggs to cook undisturbed for a minute or two, until the edges start to set.
8. Using a spatula, gently lift the edges of the omelette and tilt the skillet to let the uncooked eggs flow to the edges.
9. Continue cooking for another 2-3 minutes, or until the eggs are mostly set but still slightly runny on top.
10. If using shredded cheese, sprinkle it evenly over one half of the omelette.
11. Carefully fold the other half of the omelette over the cheese to form a half-moon shape.
12. Cook for another 1-2 minutes, or until the cheese is melted and the omelette is cooked through.
13. Slide the omelette onto a plate and serve hot.

14. You can garnish the omelette with additional cheese or fresh herbs if desired.
15. Enjoy your delicious spinach and mushroom omelette for breakfast, brunch, or any meal of the day!

Vegan Coconut Curry with Tofu

Ingredients:

- 14 oz (400g) extra firm tofu, pressed and cubed
- 2 tablespoons coconut oil or vegetable oil
- 1 onion, finely chopped
- 3 cloves garlic, minced
- 1 tablespoon fresh ginger, grated
- 2 tablespoons curry powder
- 1 teaspoon ground turmeric
- 1 teaspoon ground cumin
- 1 teaspoon ground coriander
- 1/2 teaspoon chili flakes (optional, adjust to taste)
- 1 can (14 oz) coconut milk
- 1 cup vegetable broth
- 2 cups mixed vegetables (such as bell peppers, carrots, broccoli, cauliflower, etc.), chopped
- 1 cup cherry tomatoes, halved
- 2 cups fresh spinach leaves
- Salt and pepper to taste
- Cooked rice or naan bread for serving
- Fresh cilantro for garnish (optional)
- Lime wedges for serving (optional)

Instructions:

1. Heat the coconut oil or vegetable oil in a large skillet or pot over medium heat.
2. Add the chopped onion to the skillet and sauté until softened and translucent, about 5 minutes.
3. Stir in the minced garlic and grated ginger, and cook for another minute until fragrant.
4. Add the curry powder, ground turmeric, ground cumin, ground coriander, and chili flakes (if using) to the skillet. Stir well to coat the onions with the spices and cook for 1-2 minutes to toast the spices.
5. Add the cubed tofu to the skillet and gently toss to coat with the spice mixture.
6. Pour in the coconut milk and vegetable broth, stirring to combine.
7. Bring the mixture to a simmer and cook for 10 minutes, stirring occasionally.

8. Add the chopped mixed vegetables and cherry tomatoes to the skillet. Continue to simmer for another 10-15 minutes, or until the vegetables are tender.
9. Stir in the fresh spinach leaves and cook for an additional 2-3 minutes, until the spinach is wilted.
10. Taste the curry and season with salt and pepper as needed.
11. Serve the vegan coconut curry with tofu hot over cooked rice or with naan bread on the side.
12. Garnish with fresh cilantro and serve with lime wedges for squeezing over the curry, if desired.
13. Enjoy your flavorful and nutritious vegan coconut curry with tofu!

Grilled Vegetable Skewers with Pesto Dipping Sauce

Ingredients:

For the Grilled Vegetable Skewers:

- Assorted vegetables, such as bell peppers, zucchini, cherry tomatoes, red onion, mushrooms, etc., cut into chunks
- Wooden or metal skewers

For the Pesto Dipping Sauce:

- 1 cup fresh basil leaves
- 1/4 cup pine nuts or walnuts
- 2 cloves garlic
- 1/4 cup grated Parmesan cheese (optional)
- 1/4 cup extra virgin olive oil
- Salt and pepper to taste

Instructions:

1. If using wooden skewers, soak them in water for at least 30 minutes to prevent burning on the grill.
2. Preheat your grill to medium-high heat.
3. Assemble the vegetable skewers by threading the assorted vegetable chunks onto the skewers, alternating between different vegetables.
4. Brush the assembled skewers with a little olive oil to prevent sticking on the grill.
5. Grill the vegetable skewers for 8-10 minutes, turning occasionally, or until the vegetables are tender and slightly charred.
6. While the skewers are grilling, prepare the pesto dipping sauce. In a food processor or blender, combine the fresh basil leaves, pine nuts or walnuts, garlic, and grated Parmesan cheese (if using). Pulse until finely chopped.
7. With the motor running, slowly drizzle in the extra virgin olive oil until the mixture forms a smooth paste.
8. Season the pesto dipping sauce with salt and pepper to taste, adjusting as needed.
9. Transfer the pesto dipping sauce to a small serving bowl.

10. Once the vegetable skewers are done grilling, remove them from the grill and serve hot with the pesto dipping sauce on the side.
11. Enjoy your delicious grilled vegetable skewers with pesto dipping sauce as a flavorful and nutritious appetizer or side dish!

www.ingramcontent.com/pod-product-compliance
Lightning Source LLC
LaVergne TN
LVHW081612060526
838201LV00054B/2214